DUELING SPOONS

OLIVIA HOEY & APRIL S. FIELDS

PIXELATED PUBLISHING
BUFORD GEORGIA

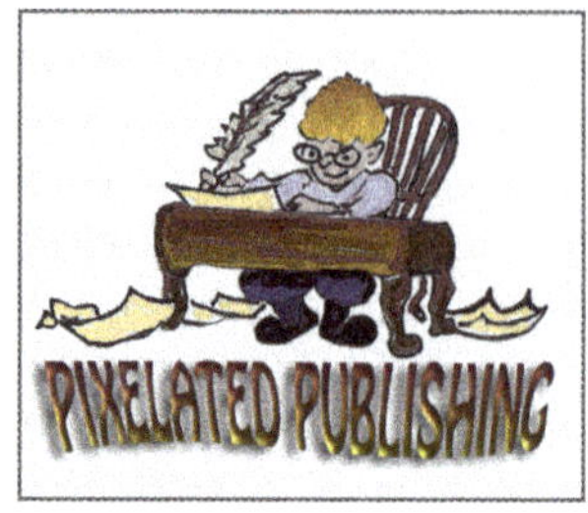

Published by Pixelated Publishing
An Imprint of Faithful Publishing
PO Box 345
Buford, Georgia 30515
faithfulpublishing@yahoo.com

ISBN 13 - 9780977988921

All recipes have been tested and deemed to be accurate in ingredients, increments, and instructions. However, since results of recipes are subject to many variables, including, but not limited to, freshness of ingredients, accurate measuring, omissions and/or unlisted substitution of ingredients and over or under cooking, therefore, we cannot guarantee perfect results for any recipe, standard or low-carb.

Photography by April S. Fields & Olivia Hoey
Dash N Dots Doodles Borders Frames - ©Meghan Bryan - www.teacherspayteachers.com

To Mom,
Thank you for everything.
~ O.H.

To my grand kids and their kids yet to be -
Imagine it, do it until you get it, even if it doesn't end up
how you imagined it.
~ A.S.F.

COMMON MEASUREMENTS

MEASURING DRY INGREDIENTS

3 teaspoons(tsp) = 1 Tablespoon (T)
4 Tablespoons = 1/4 cup
8 Tablespoons = 1/2 cup
5 1/3 Tablespoons = 1/3 cup
16 Tablespoons = 1 cup (C)
2 cups = 1 pint (pt)
4 cups = 1 quart (qt)
2 pints = 1 quart
2 quarts = 1/2 gallon
4 quarts = 1 gallon (gal)
8 quarts =1 peck (pk)
4 pecks = 1 bushel (bu)

MEASURING LIQUIDS

1/2 fluid ounce = 1 Tablespoon
1/8 cup = 1 fluid ounce
2 Tablespoons = 1/8 cup
2 fluid ounces = 4 Tablespoons
1/4 cup = 4 fluid ounces
8 Tablespoons = 1/2 cup
8 fluid ounces = 16 Tablespoons
1 cup = 8 fluid ounces
2 cups = 1 pint
32 fluid ounces = 4 cups
1 quart = 32 oz. fluid ounces
8 cups = 2 quarts
4 quarts = 1 gallon

COMMON FOOD EQUIVALENTS

1 stick butter or margarine = 1/2 cup
2 cups butter, margarine, or shortening = 1 pound
1 cup flour = 1/4 pound
4 cups flour = 1 pound
2 cups granulated sugar = 1 pound
3-1/2 cups confectioners' sugar = 1 pound
2-1/2 cups brown sugar = 1 pound
4 cups ground cocoa = 1 pound

MEEMA'S FAVORITE TOOLS & TIPS

Silpat
Wire pastry blender
More than one set of measuring spoons and cups
Small/Medium/Large mixing bowls
Thin spatula
Lots of wooden spoons
Large fry pan - used just for candy
Good heavy cookie sheet
Waxed paper/parchment paper
Plastic gloves for mixing stiff dough by hand
Candy thermometer
Wire cooling rack
Small fan to hurry cooling
Blender
Food processor
Double boiler
Assemble all ingredients and tools
Read through the recipe before you start
Always preheat oven
Always cool cakes or cookies before frosting

A word from Olivia

**"If we've almost got it, we'll get it!"
This is what Meema always says.**

Under the encouragement of this can-do motto, I grew up believing that anything is possible, even when it might look as though it can't be done. Whether it takes one last shove, a tweak here, a determined effort into the night to get an assignment completed, whatever challenges have loomed in front of me, Meema taught me to never give up (unless the bookcase simply would have to defy physics to fit in the van).

When we started this cookbook, I was still in Middle School, mouth full of braces. It was such a great idea, we thought; we'd get 'er done and sell it at the school. We didn't factor in crazy schedules, homework, soccer. One year followed another, we'd get some recipes done in the summer but even summers were a blur. Then Middle School became High School and even more scheduling issues came first, plus the demands of being involved in the school theater and one year became another until suddenly I was taller, and no braces.

We had spurts of recipe making during summers and holidays. We kept believing we'd finish before I graduated. Well, that didn't happen but, keeping with our motto, we never gave up. We realized we had beaten Julia Child's record of taking eight years to create *Joy of Cooking* and felt a little less guilt.

It's hard to believe but at this writing I'm entering my junior year in college. Though we did give up trying to plan a finish date, we kept finding a Saturday here, a Christmas vacation there, and we just kept on keeping on.

If I have learned anything from this experience, I'd have to say, first, if anything is worth doing, it's worth finishing, no matter how long it takes. Second, looking back, with the exception of the bookcase that would not fit in the van, I don't recall any thing I've set out to do that I couldn't finish because I grew up believing if I could imagine it, it was just going to happen.

But when I was still in Middle School, at the beginning of this project, I couldn't imagine being grown, in college, and working toward my own goals for my future. I didn't know that the recipes I liked would be great for college students in dorms and sorority houses. How could I have seen this cookbook in its final form being a tribute to my growing up years knowing that whatever I try, I might have to adjust my process before it's done, I might even fail several times, but so long as I just keep trying, I will succeed one way or another because *it's really the doing that matters.*

It is in the doing where success happens, where skill and determination are added into your life toolbox.

That's another Meema-ism:
It's the doing that matters.

Hope you enjoy this little cookbook as much as I am so happy to say - "It is done, we got it!"

A word from Meema

I've been a practicing "low-carber" since my husband and I started the Atkins Diet in September 1999. We reached our desired weight loss in about five months but by that time we were so thoroughly entrenched in the low-carb lifestyle we simply continued on.

Keeping it honest, we have slipped away occasionally into old habits–fast food and processed food is more convenient after all–but for the most part we have stayed true to our redesigned eating style which is quite simple and includes whole fresh foods, smaller servings, and as little sugar as possible. We don't count calories and we do not avoid "good" natural fat. The key to successful low-carbing is about eating food that satisfies. If done properly you find that you automatically eat less. Eating less, in the end, is the real secret to weight loss and maintenance. Nothing is fattening in and of itself–it's how much you eat of it that packs on the pounds. And conversely, not eating, or starving yourself, completely shuts down the metabolism which, in turn, causes weight gain over time anyway.

Nevertheless, there are other more compelling reasons to avoid empty carbs than weight loss. Type II diabetes is rampant now among adults and one of the fastest growing health problems of this era. There is nothing more heart-wrenching to me than watching a child who is glucose intolerant (or diabetic) struggle with not being able to eat sweets at school events and birthday parties. Part of my motivation to invent fun low-carb sweets–the candies and cookies especially–is founded in knowing that more and more children are adversely effected by refined sugar and even worse, high fructose corn syrup. Additionally, gluten intolerance and Celiac Disease, an auto-immune disorder exacerbated by gluten from wheat, barley and rye, is also a growing problem in children and adults. My goal has been to make it easier for parents to be able to serve or send with children healthy but equally as yummy treats so no one has to feel left out or be compelled to succumb to the temptation of the harmful sugary foods.

When my granddaughter, Olivia, an avid cook, dared me to make low-carb, low-sugar desserts that could rival her own standard favorites, how could I resist the opportunity to prove that scrumptious sweets do not have to be loaded with sugar and empty carbs?

Some of the recipes are taken from my now out of print original cookbook: ***101 Low-Carb & Sugarfree Dessert Recipes***, although I have now updated and revised them using improved ingredients, but most are new, based on my ongoing, apparently life-long, quest for satisfying, yet healthy desserts.

RANGER COOKIES

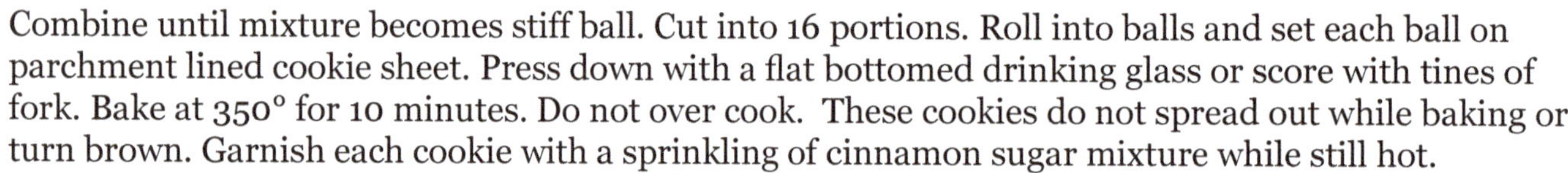

OLIVIA SAYS:

Like the Peanut Butter Cookie on pg. 10, these are made without flour. It's like a miracle!

Cream together:
- 1 cup almond butter
- 1 cup sugar
- 1 cup rice cereal
- 1 cup coconut

Mix in:
- 1 egg

Combine until mixture becomes stiff ball. Cut into 16 portions. Roll into balls and set each ball on parchment lined cookie sheet. Press down with a flat bottomed drinking glass or score with tines of fork. Bake at 350° for 10 minutes. Do not over cook. These cookies do not spread out while baking or turn brown. Garnish each cookie with a sprinkling of cinnamon sugar mixture while still hot.

Allow to cool before removing from cookie sheet.

Yield: 16 2-1/2 inch cookies

RANGER COOKIES
Low-Carb Version

Blend together:
>   2 cups almond flour
>   1 cup Whey-Low powdered
>   1/2 cup unsweetened coconut
>   1 teaspoon salt

Beat together then stir in:
>   2 egg whites
>   1 teaspoon vanilla extract

Blend together in separate bowl:
>   1 tablespoon cinnamon
>   1/2 cup Whey-Low (powdered)

Roll dough into stiff ball, chill 15 minutes. Cut dough into 24 equal parts, form into balls. Roll balls in cinnamon/Whey-Low mixture. Place balls on cookie sheet prepared with spray oil, 2" apart. Press flat with tines of fork. Bake at 350° for 10-12 minutes or until golden brown. Remove to wire racks.

Total Carbs = 72
24 Servings = 3 carbs each

PEANUT BUTTER COOKIES

OLIVIA SAYS:

Like the Ranger Cookie on pg. 8, these are gluten free!

Cream together:
    1 cup peanut butter
    1 cup sugar
    1 egg

Chill dough until stiff. Cut into 24 equal parts. Form small balls. Place on ungreased cookie sheet 2" apart. Flatten with tines of fork. Bake at 350° for 10-12 minutes. Do not over cook. Garnish with chocolate chips while still hot. Remove with thin spatula to cool on waxed paper. Cookies are fragile while still hot.

Yield: 2 dozen

Meema's Peanut Butter Cookies
Low-Carb Version

Cream together:

    1 cup peanut butter
    1 cup Whey-Low powdered
    1 cup almond flour
    1 egg
    1 teaspoon salt

Reserve until baked:

    24 Sugarfree chocolate buttons

Chill dough until stiff. Cut into 24 equal parts. Form small balls. Place on cookie sheet prepared with spray oil 2" apart. Flatten with tines of fork. Bake at 350° for 10-12 minutes. Do not over cook. Garnish with sugarfree chocolate buttons while still hot. Remove with thin spatula to cool on waxed paper. Cookies are fragile while still hot.

Note: store in refrigerator (if there are any left to store)

Total Carbs = 79
24 Servings = 3.29 carbs each

OATMEAL COOKIES

Cream together:

    1-1/4 cups butter

    1/2 cup sugar

    3/4 cup packed brown sugar

Beat in:

    1 egg

    1 teaspoon vanilla extract

Combine and add to creamed mixture:

    1-1/2 cups all-purpose flour

    1 teaspoon baking soda

    1/2 teaspoon salt

    1 teaspoon cinnamon

    1/4 teaspoon nutmeg

    1 cup chopped pecans

Add:

    3 cups quick-cooking oats

OLIVIA SAYS:

Oatmeal cookies are my mom's favorite. She adds raisins. You could also add crasins instead.

Drop by rounded tablespoonfuls 2" apart onto ungreased baking sheet. Bake at 375° for 7-9 minutes or until golden brown. Remove to wire racks.

Yield: 4-1/2 dozen

OATMEAL COOKIES
Low-Carb Version

Cream together:

    1/2 cup butter
    1 cup sugarfree maple syrup
    3/4 cup Whey-Low brown

Beat in:

    3 eggs
    1 teaspoon vanilla extract

Combine and add to creamed mixture:

    1 cup quick oats
    2 cups almond flour
    2 teaspoons baking powder
    1 teaspoon salt
    1 tablespoon cinnamon
    1/4 teaspoon nutmeg

Add:

    1 cup chopped pecans

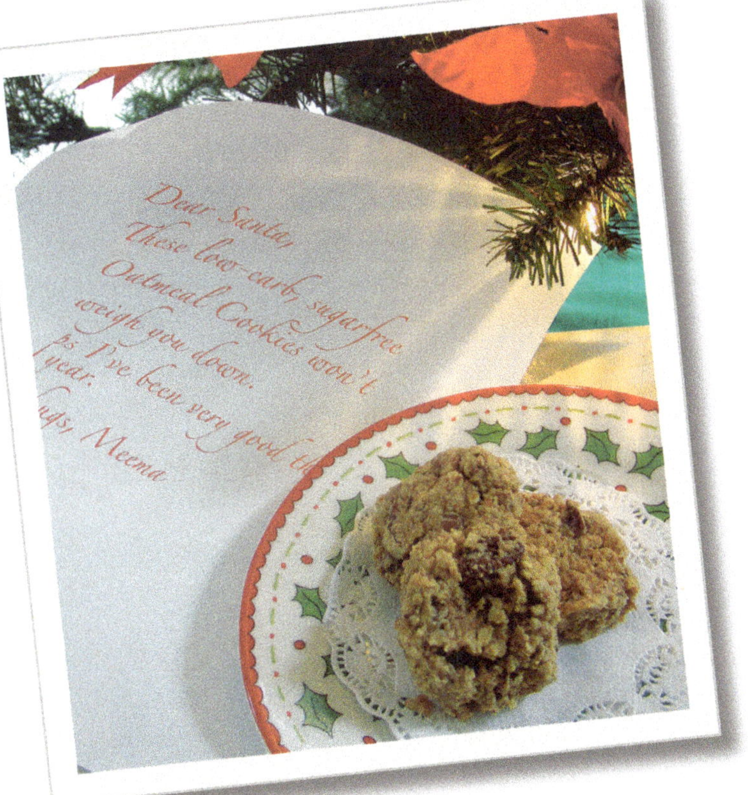

Drop by rounded tablespoonfuls 2" apart onto ungreased baking sheet. Bake at 325° for 7-9 minutes. Do not over cook. Remove to wire racks.

Total Carbs = 94
24 Servings = 3.92 carbs each

COCONUT MACAROONS

Cream together:
  16 oz. shredded coconut
  1 can (14-15 oz.) sweetened condensed milk
  2 teaspoons vanilla extract

Fill cookie press with mixture and squeeze out in 2" diameter balls 2" apart onto baking sheet prepared with spray oil. Bake at 350° for 8 minutes or until golden brown. Remove to wire racks.

Yield: 3-4 dozen

Joy! Coconut Cookies
Low-Carb Version

Combine:
- 1 cup almond flour
- 1 cup Whey-Low powdered
- 1/2 cup unsweetened coconut flour
- 1/2 teaspoon coconut extract

Reserve for garnish:
- 24 sugarfree chocolate buttons
- 24 almond slivers

Chill dough 20-30 minutes. Cut chilled dough into 24 equal parts. Form balls and place 2" apart onto baking sheet prepared with spray oil. Bake at 350° for 7-9 minutes. Do not over cook, they will not brown. Garnish with chocolate buttons and almond slivers while still hot. Remove to wire racks. Note: cookies are fragile when hot.

Total Carbs = 64.70
24 Servings = 2.70 carbs each

OrangeCran Cookies

Combine:

    1 package orange cake mix
    1/2 cup cooking oil
    2 eggs
    1 teaspoon grated orange peel
    1/2 cup craisins

Reserve to garnish:

    orange cake frosting
    orange sprinkles

Drop by rounded tablespoonfuls 2" apart onto ungreased baking sheet. Bake at 350° for 7-10 minutes. Remove to wire racks. Frost when cool.

Yield: 6 dozen

ORANGE COOKIES
Low-Carb Version

Blend together:

    2 cups almond flour

    1 cup Whey-Low powdered

    2 teaspoons baking powder

    1 teaspoon salt

    2 teaspoon orange rind

    1 packet orange drink powder (sugarfree)

Beat in:

    2 eggs

    1/2 cup butter

    1 tablespoon lemon juice

Make and chill glaze:

    1 cup Whey-Low powdered

    1 tablespoon lemon juice

    1 teaspoon orange extract

    3 tablespoons butter

    2 drops orange food color

Chill dough for 30 minutes. Cut chilled dough into 24 equal parts. Shape into balls and place 2" apart onto baking sheet prepared with spray oil. Bake at 350° for 10 minutes. Do not brown. Remove to wire racks. Pipe glaze onto cooled cookies with pastry bag.

Total Carbs = 111

24 Servings = 4.62 each

Thumbprint Cookies

Cream together:
- 1/2 cup shortening
- 1 cup packed brown sugar
- 1/2 cup sugar

Beat in:
- 1 egg
- 1 teaspoon vanilla extract

Combine and add to creamed mixture:
- 1 cup all-purpose flour
- 1/2 teaspoon baking soda
- 1/4 teaspoon baking powder
- 1/2 teaspoon salt
- 2 tablespoons dry cocoa powder

Add:
- 1-1/4 cups quick-cooking oats

Use chocolate frosting on pg. 19 substituting powdered sugar to fill centers.

Form into balls and place 2" apart onto ungreased baking sheet. Press center with back of measuring spoon. Bake at 325° for 8-10 minutes. Remove to wire racks. Fill centers with frosting when cooled.

Yield: 3 dozen

Thumbprint Cookies
Low-Carb Version

Cream together:
> 4 oz. cream cheese
> 1/4 cup butter

Beat in:
> 2 eggs
> 1 teaspoon vanilla extract

Combine and add to creamed mixture:
> 2 cups almond flour
> 1 cup Whey-Low brown
> 1/2 teaspoon salt
> 1 cup finely chopped pecans

Icing:
> 4 oz. cream cheese
> 1/4 cup butter
> 1 teaspoon vanilla
> 1 cup Whey-Low (powdered
> green and red food color

Chill dough 30 minutes. Form chilled dough into balls and place 2" apart onto baking sheet prepared with spray oil. Press into center with back of measuring spoon to make dent. Bake at 325° for 9-10 minutes. Remove to wire racks. Fill centers with frosting or sugarfree chocolate buttons.

Total Carbs = 136.20
30 Servings = 4.54 carbs each

Blonde Brownies

Cream together:

    2/3 cup butter

    2 cup packed brown sugar

Beat in:

    2 eggs

    2 teaspoons vanilla extract

Combine and add to creamed mixture:

    2 cups all-purpose flour

    1 teaspoon baking soda

    1 teaspoon baking powder

    1/2 teaspoon salt

Add:

    1 (7 oz.) bag butterscotch morsels

    1/2 cup finely chopped nuts (optional)

Drop by rounded tablespoonfuls 2" apart onto ungreased baking sheet. Or press dough into glass pie pan prepared with spray oil. Bake at 350° for 7-9 minutes or until golden brown or 20-25 minutes in pie pan. Remove to wire racks.

Yield: 2 dozen cookies or 10 large slices

BLONDE BROWNIE STARS
Low-Carb Version

Cream together:
- 4 oz. cream cheese
- 1/4 cup butter
- 1 cup Whey-Low powdered

Beat in:
- 1 egg
- 2 teaspoons vanilla extract

Combine and add to creamed mixture:
- 2 cups almond flour
- 1/2 teaspoon salt

Icing (optional):
- 4 oz. cream cheese
- 1/2 cup Whey-Low (powdered)
- Almond slices

Chill dough 20-30 minutes. Divide dough into 12 equal balls. Press each ball evenly into star-shaped bake pan prepared with spray oil. Bake at 350° for 12-14 minutes. Do not overcook they do not brown. Remove to wire racks. Ice and garnish when cool.

Total Carbs = 103.6
12 Servings = 8.63 carbs each

Lemon Squares

Olivia says:

Ooey gooey
goodness!

Combine for crust:
> 1/4 cup sugar
> 3 tablespoons butter
> 1 cup all-purpose flour

Combine well into batter for topping:
> 3 eggs
> 3/4 cup sugar
> 2 teaspoons grated lemon rind
> 1/3 cup fresh lemon juice
> 3 tablespoons all-purpose flour
> 1/2 teaspoon baking powder
> 1/8 teaspoon salt

Reserve to garnish:
> 2 tablespoons powdered sugar

Press prepared crust mixture evenly into bottom of 8" baking pan. It will be crumbly. Bake at 350° for 10 minutes. Remove from oven. Pour prepared topping batter over crust. Bake at 350° for 20-25 minutes or until set. Cool on wire rack. Sift powdered sugar on top when cooled.

Yield: 8-12 depending on cut

LEMON SQUARES
LOW-CARB VERSION

Combine for crust:
- 1/4 cup all-purpose flour
- 1/2 cup almond flour
- 1/2 cup Whey-Low powdered
- 1/2 cup mayonnaise (not salad dressing)

Combine well into batter for topping:
- 2 eggs
- 1/2 cup Whey-Low powdered
- 1 teaspoons grated lemon rind
- 1 tablespoon corn starch
- 4 tablespoons lemon juice
- 1/2 teaspoon baking powder
- 1/2 teaspoon salt

Reserve to garnish:
- 2 tablespoons Whey-Low powdered

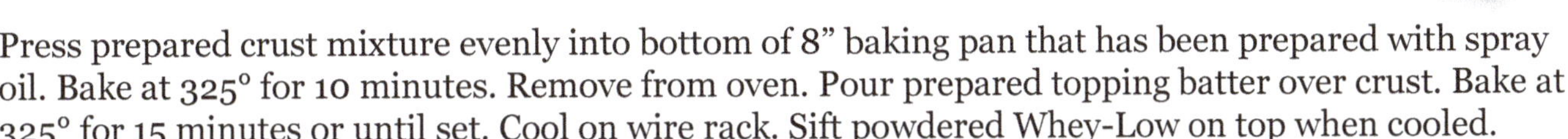

Press prepared crust mixture evenly into bottom of 8" baking pan that has been prepared with spray oil. Bake at 325° for 10 minutes. Remove from oven. Pour prepared topping batter over crust. Bake at 325° for 15 minutes or until set. Cool on wire rack. Sift powdered Whey-Low on top when cooled.

Total Carbs = 82.95
8 Servings = 10.37 carbs each

Maple Pecan Chewies

Cream together:
   1 tablespoon butter
   1 tablespoon maple syrup
   1/2 teaspoon maple extract
   1 egg
Combine and add to creamed mixture:
   1 box Jiffy Cake mix
   1/4 cup brown sugar
   1/4 cup pecans, coarsely chopped (approx. 4 oz.)

Spoon mixture into mini muffin cup liners in two mini-muffin tins.
Press pecan piece into top of each.

Bake for 10-11 minutes at 350˚. Allow to cool.

Yield: 2 dozen

Maple Pecan Bites
Low-Carb Version

Cream together:
> 1/2 cup butter (1 stick)
> 1 cup Whey-Low powdered

Beat in:
> 1 egg yolk
> 1 teaspoon maple extract

Combine and add to creamed mixture:
> 1 cup almond flour
> 1 cup pecan meal

Reserve to garnish:
> 24 pecan halves

Chill dough for 20 minutes. Divide chilled dough into 24 pieces, then form 24 balls. Place each ball in mini muffin cups, lined with paper cup. Bake at 325° for 9-11 minutes or until just turning golden. Remove to wire racks.

Total Carbs = 84
24 Servings = 3.5 carbs each

Macadamia Chocolate Chip Cookies

Cream together:

    1/2 cup butter (1 stick)

    1/3 cup sugar

    1/3 cup packed brown sugar

Beat in:

    1 egg

    1 teaspoon vanilla extract

Combine and add to creamed mixture:

    1-1/8 cups all-purpose flour

    1/2 teaspoon baking soda

    1/2 teaspoon salt

Add:

    1 cup chopped macadamia nuts

    1 cup semisweet chocolate chips

Chill dough 20-30 minutes. Divide dough into 24 equal pieces. Form balls and place 2" apart onto baking sheet prepared with spray oil. Bake at 375° for 10-12 minutes or until golden brown. Remove to wire racks.

Yield: 2 dozen

Macadamia Chocolate Chip Cookies
Low-Carb Version

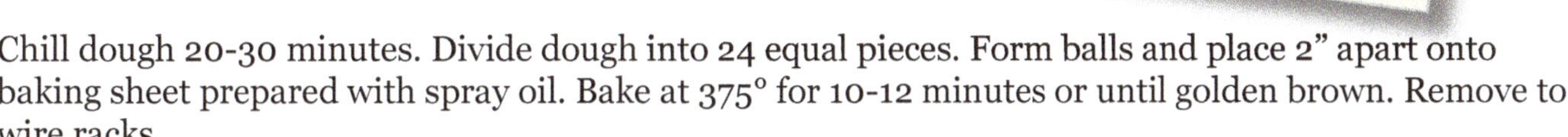

Cream together:

    1/2 cup butter (4 oz. = 1 stick)

    1 cup Whey-Low brown

Beat in:

    1 egg

    1 teaspoon vanilla extract

Combine and add to creamed mixture:

    2 cups almond flour

    1/2 teaspoon baking soda

    1/2 teaspoon salt

Add:

    1 cup chopped macadamia nuts

    1/2 cup semisweet chocolate chips

Chill dough 20-30 minutes. Divide dough into 24 equal pieces. Form balls and place 2" apart onto baking sheet prepared with spray oil. Bake at 375° for 10-12 minutes or until golden brown. Remove to wire racks.

Total Carbs = 94

24 Servings = 3.92 carbs each

SHORT BREAD

Cream together:
>   2 cups butter (4 sticks)
>   1 cup packed brown sugar

Add:
>   4-1/2 cups all-purpose flour

Mix ingredients well. Sprinkle cutting board with flour. Knead for 5 minutes, adding enough flour to make a soft dough. Press into shaped cookie pan. Bake at 325° for 10 minutes. Remove to wire racks. Cool completely. Remove by gently pushing tip of sharp knife at one edge, then lift out.

Yield: 2 - 2-1/2 dozen

MACADAMIA SHORT BREAD
Low-Carb Version

Cream together:

  1/2 cup butter (1 stick)
  1 cup Whey-Low brown

Add:

  2 tablespoons all-purpose flour
  1 tablespoon cornstarch
  2 cups macadamia nut flour (almond flour can be substituted)

Mix ingredients well. Press dough evenly into bake dish prepared with spray oil. Bake at 275° for 30 minutes. Center will be soft until it cools. Cool in the bake dish. Cut 16 equal pieces. Remove with sharp spatula.

Keep refrigerated.

Total Carbs = 81.18
16 Servings = 5.07 carbs each

Caramel Corn

Melt in large fry pan over medium heat:

    1/2 cup butter (1 stick)

Add:

    1 cup sugar

Cook and stir until butter and sugar blend. When mixture comes to a foaming boil, begin timing. Cook for 2 minutes or until mixture turns brown. Do not over cook.

Pour over 4 cups of popped corn. Be sure to remove any unpopped kernels first. Stir until all corn is coated. Pour out onto Silpat or aluminum foil or other non-stick surface. Allow to cool.

Yield: 8 servings

CARAMEL CORN
LOW-CARB VERSION

Melt in large fry pan over medium heat:

    1/2 cup butter (1 stick)

Add:

    1 cup Whey-Low powdered

Cook and stir until butter and sugar blend. When mixture comes to a foaming boil, begin timing. Cook for 2 minutes or until mixture turns brown. Do not over cook.

Pour over 4 cups of popped corn. Be sure to remove any unpopped kernels first. Stir until all corn is coated. Pour out onto Silpat or aluminum foil or other not stick surface. Allow to cool.

Total Carbs = 80.5
8 Servings = 10.06 carbs each

Pecan Brittle

Melt in large fry pan over medium heat:

    1/2 cup butter (1 stick)

Add:

    1 cup sugar

Cook and stir until butter and sugar blend. When mixture comes to a foaming boil, begin timing. Cook for 2 minutes or until mixture turns brown. Do not over cook. Turn off heat.

Stir in:

    1 cup chopped pecans

Stir until all nuts are coated. Pour out onto Silpat or aluminum foil or other not stick surface. Allow to cool. Break into pieces.

Yield: Various depending on piece size

Butter Pecan Brittle
Low-Carb Version

Melt in large fry pan over medium heat:

    1/2 cup butter (1 stick)

Add:

    1 cup Whey-Low powdered

Cook and stir until butter and Whey-Low blend. When mixture comes to a foaming boil, begin timing. Cook for 2 minutes or until mixture turns brown. Do not over cook. Turn off heat.

Stir in:

    1 cup chopped pecans

Stir until all nuts are coated. Pour out onto Silpat or aluminum foil or other not stick surface. Allow to cool. Break into pieces.

Total Carbs = 56
24 pieces = 2.33 carbs each

ORANGE BALLS

 **OLIVIA SAYS:**

When you bite into one of these, it starts out tart and ends up mild sweet.

Cream together:
> 2 boxes orange gelatin dessert mix less 3 tablespoons
> 1 cup finely shredded coconut
> 1 can sweetened evaporated milk

Reserve for garnish:
> remaining dry orange gelatin mix

Chill dough for 30 minutes. Divide dough into 48 pieces. Roll each piece into small ball. Roll ball into dry gelatin mix. Keep refrigerated. If serving as a party dessert, put each ball in paper candy cup.

Yield: 4 dozen

ORANGE BALLS
LOW-CARB VERSION

Melt in double-boiler or microwave and set aside:
> 3/4 cup food grade, unsweetened cocoa butter

Combine in separate bowl:
> 2 tablespoons sugarfree powdered orange drink mix
> 1 tablespoon unflavored gelatin
> 2 cups almond flour
> 1/2 cup unsweetened coconut
> 1 cup Whey-Low powdered

Add:
> 1/2 cup orange sugarfree syrup
> 1 teaspoon vanilla

Mix and reserve for garnish:
> sugarfree powdered orange drink mix
> unsweetened coconut

Mix melted cocoa butter into remaining blended ingredients. Divide dough into 48 pieces. Roll each piece into small ball. Roll ball into dry drink mix/coconut mixture. Keep refrigerated. If serving as a party dessert, put each ball in paper candy cup.

Total Carbs = 48
48 servings = 1 carb each

Easy Creamy Fudge

Fudge is a noun, a verb,
an interjection, and delicious!
~Terri Guillemets

Cream together:

8 oz. cream cheese
1/2 cup melted butter
1 teaspoon vanilla

Beat in:

4 cups powdered sugar, one cup at a time
2/3 cup baking cocoa
1 teaspoon salt

Reserve to garnish:

1 cup chopped nuts - walnuts or pecans

Press mixture into ungreased 8X8 glass dish. Garnish with nuts. Chill completely. Cut into 16 squares. Keep refrigerated.

Yield: 16

CREAMY FUDGE
LOW-CARB VERSION

Melt in double-boiler:

>1 cup food grade, unsweetened cocoa butter
>
>2 blocks unsweetened baker's chocolate chipped or grated

Remove from heat allow to cool slightly.

Cream together:

>8 oz. cream cheese
>
>2 cups Whey-Low powdered
>
>2 tsp vanilla extract

Add creamed mixture to warm cocoa butter with electric mixer until batter is smooth, shiny and just beginning to thicken.

Stir in:

>1/2 cup chopped walnuts

Pour into an 8X8 glass dish lined with waxed paper. Chill completely. Cut into 36 squares. Keep refrigerated.

Total Carbs = 104

36 Servings = 6.5 carbs each

Candied Walnuts

Stir together in heavy sauce pan over medium heat:

>   1/2 cup sour cream
>   1 cup brown sugar

Cook to soft ball stage (242°) Remove from heat.
Add:

>   1-1/2 teaspoons vanilla
>   2 cups walnut pieces

Stir until walnuts are well coated. Turn out onto Silpat or waxed paper. While still warm, separate into portions. Serve in foil mini muffin or candy cups.

Yield: 24

CANDIED WALNUTS
Low-Carb Version

Heat in heavy sauce pan over medium heat:

    1/2 cup sour cream
    1 cup Whey-Low (brown)

Cook to soft ball stage (242°) Remove from heat.
Add:

    1-1/2 teaspoons vanilla
    2 cups walnut pieces

Stir until walnuts are well coated. Turn out onto Silpat or waxed paper. While still warm, separate into portions. Serve in foil mini muffin or candy cups.

Total Carbs = 48
24 Servings = 2 carbs each

MEEMA SAYS:

The only difference between these recipes is the sugar. By using Whey-Low you can reduce the total carbohydrate count from 192 to 48. They look and taste the same.

Spiced Nuts

Shake together in 2 quart food saver plastic bag:

 1/2 cup sugar
 1 teaspoon cinnamon
 1/4 teaspoon ground nutmeg
 1/4 teaspoon ground cloves
 1/2 teaspoon salt

Beat until foamy:

 1 egg white

Coat:

 3 cups pecan halves

Toss coated nuts into spice/sugar mixture. Spread out on cookie sheet that has been prepared with spray oil. Bake 250° for 45 minutes or until sugar begins to caramelize. Turn out onto Silpat or waxed paper. Break apart into individual nuts while still warm.

Yield: Depends on number of nuts

SPICED NUTS
LOW-CARB VERSION

Shake together in 2 quart food saver plastic bag:

    1/2 cup Whey-Low powdered

    1 teaspoon cinnamon

    1/4 teaspoon ground nutmeg

    1/4 teaspoon ground cloves

Beat until foamy:

    1 egg white

Coat:

    3 cups walnut halves in egg white

Toss coated nuts into spice/sugar mixture. Spread out on cookie sheet that has been prepared with spray oil. Bake 325° for 10 minutes or until sugar begins to caramelize. Turn out onto Silpat or waxed paper. Break apart into individual nuts while still warm.

Total Carbs = 12

24 servings = 1/2 carb each

BUCKEYES

OLIVIA SAYS:

The original Buckeye recipe came from my great grandmother, Mary Fields, who made these every Christmas. I have taken some shortcuts with more modern ingredients, but the taste is still the same melt in your mouth delicious.

Cream together:

    1 cup peanut butter
    1/2 cup butter (1 stick) softened

Beat in:

    1 teaspoon maple extract

Combine and add to creamed mixture:

    2 cups almond flour
    1 cup powdered sugar

Knead dough until smooth. Form into ball and chill in refrigerator for 30 minutes.

Melt in microwave:

    1 bag (16 oz.) milk chocolate candy making wafers.

Cut chilled dough into 48 equal pieces. Roll into small balls. Place each ball in decorative mini muffin cup. Spoon melted chocolate onto each ball. Allow to firm. Chill.

Yield: 4 dozen

BUCKEYES
Low-Carb Version

Cream together:
>	1 cup peanut butter
>	1/2 cup butter (1 stick)

Beat in:
>	2 tablespoons rum (optional)
>	1 teaspoon maple extract

Combine and add to creamed mixture:
>	2 cups almond flour
>	1 cup Whey-Low (powdered)

Roll into ball and refrigerate.

Melt in double-boiler:
>	1 oz. semi-sweet baker's chocolate
>	1/4 block paraffin wax
>	1 cup food grade unsweetened cocoa butter

Add:
>	1 cup Whey-Low (powdered)

Stir together until smooth. Turn off burner. Cut chilled dough into 48 pieces. Roll into small balls. Dip one ball at a time into the warm chocolate mixture using a slotted spoon or a bamboo skewer. Place ball onto large cookie sheet that has been covered with waxed paper. Allow to firm. Chill.

Total Carbs = 61
48 Servings = 1.28 carbs each

TRUFFLES

Mix together into soft dough ball and chill:
> 1 8 oz. package cream cheese
> 1 large box (5.9 oz.) Instant Chocolate
> Pudding Mix (dry)

Stir together to make chocolate sauce coating:
> 4 oz. softened cream cheese
> (soften in microwave but do not over heat)
> 1/2 cup powdered sugar
> 1 tablespoon dry unsweetened cocoa powder

Reserve to finish coat:
> finely chopped nuts
> coconut
> sprinkles
> crushed peppermint candy

When ready to coat, cut dough ball in half, then into quarters, and continue dividing to make 24 to 36 portions. Roll each small piece into a ball. Using two teaspoons dip small ball into chocolate sauce, then any other finishing layer of choice, coconut, finely chopped nuts, chocolate sprinkles, crushed peppermint. Place in individual candy cups. Chill.

> Variation on the chocolate sauce:
> Add: tablespoon peanut butter or any flavor extract like Rum, coconut or orange.
> Keep refrigerated.

Yield: 2-3 dozen

TRUFFLES
LOW-CARB VERSION

> THERE ARE FOUR BASIC FOOD
> GROUPS: MILK CHOCOLATE, DARK
> CHOCOLATE, WHITE CHOCOLATE,
> AND CHOCOLATE TRUFFLES.
> ~AUTHOR UNKNOWN

Melt together in top of double-boiler:
    1/2 cup food grade cocoa butter
    1 block semi-sweet baker's chocolate grated
Add:
    2 teaspoon vanilla extract
    1/2 cup almond butter
Combine in separate bowl:
    2 cups almond flour
    1 cup Whey-Low powdered
    1/2 cup unsweetened coconut
    1/2 cup pecans finely chopped
Reserve for garnish:
    2 tablespoons cocoa bake powder
    1/2 cup Whey-Low (powdered)
    1/2 cup unsweetened coconut

Mix together the melted cocoa with the remaining mixture until it is a stiff dough. Chill in refrigerator. Cut chilled dough into 48 pieces. Roll into small balls. Roll one ball at a time into the cocoa/coconut mixture. Place on cookie sheet that has been covered with waxed paper. Allow to firm. Chill.

Total Carbs = 60
48 Servings = 1.25 carbs each

STRAWBERRY JEWELS

Cream together:

    2 boxes strawberry gelatin dessert mix
    1 cup finely shredded coconut
    1 can sweetened evaporated milk
    1/2 cup finely chopped pecans

Reserve for garnish:

    red and green decorative sugar crystals

Chill dough for 30 minutes. Divide dough into 48 pieces. Roll each piece into small ball. Form ball into strawberry shape. Dip flat end in green sugar crystals. Roll remaining strawberry in red sugar crystals. Garnish with almond "stem" and allow to dry on cookie sheet covered with waxed paper.

Yield: 4 dozen

STRAWBERRY JEWELS
Low-Carb Version

Melt in double-boiler or microwave:
    1 cup food grade unsweetened cocoa butter
Combine in separate bowl and add to cocoa butter:
    2 cups almond flour
    1 cup Whey-Low (powdered)
    3 packs of unsweetened flavored drink powder
Add:
    1 cup vanilla sugarfree syrup
Reserve for garnish:
    red and green decorative sugar crystals
    almond slivers (optional)

Mix all ingredients into soft dough. Do not chill. Divide into 36 small balls. Form each ball into shape of strawberry. Dip flat end in green sugar crystals. Roll remaining strawberry in red sugar crystals. Garnish with almond sliver "stem" and allow to dry on cookie sheet covered with waxed paper.

Total Carbs = 74.4
36 Servings = 2.07 carbs each

CHOCOLATE CHEWIES

Heat in heavy sauce pan until full boil for 2 minutes.
- 1/2 cup heavy cream
- 1 cup powdered sugar
- 1 teaspoon vanilla extract

Remove from heat: Stir in:
- 1 cup nonfat dry milk powder
- 1/2 cup dry baking cocoa

Reserve for finishing:
- 1 tablespoon cornstarch in a quart sized plastic saver bag

Stir quickly until it becomes stiff dough. Turn out onto Silpat or waxed paper allow to cool. When cool, roll out with palms into a long rope (like modeling dough). Cut with clean kitchen shears into sections and continue rolling sections into smaller ropes until they are less than 1/2" thick. Cut into bite-sized pieces. Drop pieces into plastic bag with cornstarch. Shake to coat. Wrap individual pieces in tissue paper for gifting or store in air-tight container in refrigerator.

Yield: 4 dozen

Chocolate Chewies
Low-Carb Version

Heat in heavy sauce pan until full boil for 2 minutes. Remove from heat:

    1/2 cup heavy cream

    1 cup Whey-Low powdered

Stir in:

    1 teaspoon vanilla extract

Stir in:

    1 cup Whey Protein Isolate (sugarfree protein drink powder)

    1/2 cup dry baking cocoa

Reserve for finishing:

    1 tablespoon cornstarch in a quart sized plastic saver bag

Stir quickly until it becomes stiff dough. Turn out onto Silpat or waxed paper allow to cool. When cool, roll out with palms into a long rope (like modeling dough). Cut with clean kitchen shears into sections and continue rolling sections into smaller ropes until they are less than 1/2" thick. Cut into bite-sized pieces. Drop pieces into plastic bag with cornstarch. Shake to coat. Wrap individual pieces in tissue paper for gifting or store in air-tight container in refrigerator.

Total Carbs = 77

48 Servings = 1.60 carbs each

TURTLES

 OLIVIA SAYS:

Okay, so my version of Turtle Candy does not look anything like turtles but they taste just as good and are way easier to make.

Unwrap 36 caramel candies. Heat in medium bowl in microwave until melted.
Fill 24 paper-lined mini-muffin cup bake pan:
    Bottom - pecans
    Middle - spoon of caramel
    Top - 1 chocolate candy making button

Bake at 350° for 10 minutes or until chocolate button is melty. Remove from oven and immediately top with another chocolate button. Allow to cool to room temperature then chill.

Yield: 2 dozen

Skillet Turtle Candy
Low-Carb Version

Melt in a double boiler over medium heat:
- 1/4 block paraffin wax (Gulf Wax)
- 1 oz. unsweetened baking chocolate

Add:
- 1 cup Whey-Low Powdered
- 2 tablespoons heavy cream

Stir until creamy. Turn off heat.

Blend in large heavy skillet:
- 1 cup Whey-Low Gold
- 1/2 cup sour cream

Cook until bubbly, then cook 2 more minutes. Remove from heat.

Add and coat:
- 2 cups chopped pecans

Pour mixture onto Silpat or waxed paper. While still hot, cover with chocolate and divide into individual portions. Or, fill candy cups with coated pecans and then spoon chocolate over each one.

Allow to cool. Chill.

Total Carbs = 60
12 Servings = 5 carbs each

Cream Cheese Pie Pastry

Cream together:

 8 oz. cream cheese

 1/2 cup butter

 1 egg

Combine and add to creamed mixture:

 1 cup all-purpose flour

 1/2 teaspoon salt

Work ingredients together until well blended. Shape into ball and chill for 15-30 minutes. Press chilled dough into 9" baking dish prepared with spray oil. Bake at 325° for 15-20 minutes or until just beginning to brown. Yield: 1 pie crust.

Yield: 8 Servings = 11 carbs each (without filling)

CREAM CHEESE PIE PASTRY
Low-Carb Version

Cream together until there are no lumps left:
    4 oz. cream cheese
    1/2 cup butter (1 stick)
Add and blend well:
    1 egg
Combine and add to creamed mixture:
    2 cups almond flour
    1/2 cup Tapioca flour
    1/2 teaspoon salt

MEEMA SAYS:

This pastry crust will brown quickly in the oven. If you are baking the crust with the filling you will find the crust cooks faster than the filling. Remove the pie as soon as the edges begin to brown and finish in the microwave. Usually takes about 5 minutes but test every two minutes until the center is firm.

Work ingredients together until well blended. Shape into ball and chill for 15-30 minutes. Press chilled dough into baking dish. Pierce with fork tines to prevent puffing. Bake at 325° for 20-25 minutes or until just beginning to brown.

Total Carbs = 39
10 Servings = 3.9 carbs each (without filling)

Peach Cobbler

Pie...it fills the cracks of the heart. Go away, pain.
~Kevin James, Mall Cop

Prepare and set aside:
> 1 recipe Cream Cheese Pastry (pg. 52)

Mix together:
> 2 cans peaches (drained)
> 1 tablespoon cinnamon
> 1/4 cup sugar

Prepare 9" bake dish with pastry. Push dough up slightly above top edge. Fill evenly with coated peaches. Fold edges of dough back down over peaches. Bake at 375° for 25 minutes or until center is bubbly and dough is just beginning to brown.

Yield: 18-12 servings

EASY AS PIE COBBLER
LOW-CARB VERSION

Prepare and set aside:

    1 recipe Cream Cheese Pastry (Low-Carb) (pg. 53)

Mix together:

    2 cans low-sugar (lite) peaches (drained)
    1 tablespoon cinnamon
    1/4 cup Whey-Low (powdered)

Prepare 9" bake dish with pastry. Push dough up slightly above top edge. Fill evenly with coated peaches. Fold edges of dough back down over peaches. Bake at 350° for 25-35 minutes or until center is bubbly and dough is just beginning to brown.

Total Carbs = 86.75 (including pastry)
8 Servings = 10.84 carbs each

Key Lime Pie

Prepare and bake a 9" pie crust or use a ready-to-fill graham crust.
In a large bowl combine:
    14 oz. can sweetened condensed milk
    6 oz. can frozen limeade concentrate (not thawed)
    1 cup heavy cream
Reserve to garnish:
    zest of lime

Beat the mixture with an electric mixer until light and fluffy. Pour filling into baked pie shell. refrigerate until set. Serve topped with whipped cream and zest of lime.

Yield: 8-10 slices

KEY LIME TART
Low-Carb Version

Prepare and bake a 9" low carb pie crust (pg. 54):
Combine in medium sauce pan and heat until melted. Remove from heat:

    8 oz. block cream cheese
    1 cup heavy cream
    1 cup Whey-Low powdered

Add:

    4 tablespoons lime juice

Soften 1 tablespoon unflavored gelatin in 1 cup vanilla sugarfree syrup. Bring to boiling point.
Fold into cream cheese mixture. Allow to cool but do not chill. Pour cooled mixture into baked pie shell.
Refrigerate until set. Serve with whipped cream and lime zest garnish.

Total Carbs = 60
12 Servings = 5 carbs each

FRUIT PIZZA

Line an ungreased 14" pizza pan with sugar cookie dough. Bake 10-12 minutes or until light brown. Remove and allow to cool.

Cream together and spread over baked cookie dough:

>   8 oz. cream cheese
>
>   1/3 cup sugar
>
>   1 teaspoon vanilla extract

Combine in small sauce pan over low heat:

>   1/2 cup fruit preserves of choice
>
>   1 tablespoon of water

Arrange fruit of choice on cream cheese. Brush heated fruit glaze over fruit. Chill.

Yield: 10-12 slices

FRUIT PIZZA
LOW-CARB VERSION

Line an ungreased 14" pizza pan with Low-Carb Cream Cheese Pastry (pg 53). Bake 10-12 minutes or until light brown. Remove and allow to cool.

Cream together and spread over baked cookie dough:

    8 oz. cream cheese

    1/2 cup Whey-Low (powdered)

    1 teaspoon vanilla extract

Combine in small sauce pan over low heat:

    1/2 cup sugarfree or pure fruit preserves of choice

    1 tablespoon of water

Arrange fruit of choice on cream cheese. Brush heated fruit glaze over fruit. Refrigerate.

Total Carbs = based on combination of ingredients

EASY CHERRY PARFAIT

OLIVIA SAYS:

This started out as pie. It didn't set up so instead of throwing away perfectly good ingredients, I made it into a spoonable dessert instead. Classic example of not giving up and finding a workaround.

Cream together:
    16 oz. cream cheese (softened)
    14 oz. can sweetened condensed milk
    1 tablespoon vanilla extract
Layer mixture with:
    graham cracker crumbs
    cherry pie filling

Chill in refrigerator until set. Garnish with whipped cream and a pinch of graham cracker crumbs.

Yield: 8-10 parfaits depending on stemware used

CHERRY CHEESECAKE
Low-Carb Version

Combine in blender:
>6 eggs
>16 oz. cream cheese
>1/2 cup vanilla sugarfree syrup

Reserve to garnish:
>1 can Lucky Leaf Lite Cherry Pie Filling

Blend until completely homogenized. Pour into a 9" glass pie plate that has been prepared with spray oil. Bake at 350° for 50 minute or until a knife inserted in center comes out clean. This pie will swell up in the heat of the oven and then shrink back when cool. Before serving, top with cherry pie filling and whipped cream.

Total Carbs = 48
8 Servings = 6 carbs each

Strawberry Tarts

Olivia says:

Keep certain things on hand,
like the boxed tartlett shells,
and you will always be able to whip
up a quick dessert. Cream cheese
and gelatin are also
good things
to have.

Cream together:

    1 8 oz. block of cream cheese
    1/4 cup heavy cream
    1/4 teaspoon strawberry extract
    1 box strawberry gelatin (large)

Whip with hand mixer until smooth.

Drop by teaspoonfuls into ready-made tartlett shells, or use the Cream Cheese Pastry recipe on pg. 52 to make your own tartletts (prebaked).

Garnish with strawberry jam, almond slivers, sprinkles, or whatever you have on hand. You can use this recipe with different gelatins for different flavors.

Yield: 32

STRAWBERRY TART
LOW-CARB VERSION

Cream together:

>   4 oz. cream cheese
>   1/2 cup butter (1 stick)

Combine and add to creamed mixture:

>   1-1/2 cups almond flour
>   1/2 teaspoon vanilla
>   1 tablespoon cornstarch
>   1 tablespoon unsweetened coconut
>   1 tablespoon pecan meal

Knead into dough and press into non-stick release type tart pan. Pierce in several places. Bake at 325° for 15 minutes. Remove and allow to cool in pan.

Cream together:

>   16 oz. cream cheese
>   1 cup vanilla sugarfree syrup

Pour filling into cooled tart shell. Arrange cut strawberry halves on top.

Combine in small sauce pan on medium heat just to boil:

>   1 cup peach flavored sugarfree syrup
>   2 tablespoons lemon juice
>   1 tablespoon cornstarch

Allow glaze to cool before coating strawberries. Refrigerate until ready to serve. Release tart from pan and arrange on decorative plate.

Total Carbs = 56.6
12 Servings = 4.72 carbs each

CHOCOLATE MOCHA PIE

Line a deep dish pie plate with Oreo Cookies.
Filling:
Combine in medium sauce pan:

      1 large box (6 oz.) chocolate pudding
      1 small package unflavored gelatin
      3 cups milk
      1 8 oz block cream cheese cut into small cubes

Bring to rolling boil and stir while boiling until cream cheese is melted and blended. Remove from heat and allow to cool. Tip: quick cool the mixture by setting the pan in a large pan of ice.

When cool fill the Oreo Cookie crust with mixture and refrigerate until chilled.
Serve garnished with whipped cream or chocolate syrup drizzled over slice.

Yield: 8 slices

COCOMOCHA PIE
Low-Carb Version

Prepare 9" pie crust using the Cream Cheese Pastry (pg. 53).

Combine in blender:

- 8 oz. cream cheese
- 4 eggs
- 2 tablespoons dry baking cocoa
- 1/4 cup heavy whipping cream
- 1 cup vanilla sugarfree syrup
- 1 tablespoon dry instant coffee
- 1/2 cup Whey-Low powdered

Mix and reserve to garnish:

- 4 oz. cream cheese
- 1/2 cup butter (1 stick)
- 1/2 cup Whey-Low powdered
- 1 tablespoon dry instant coffee
- 1 tablespoon dry cocoa powder
- 1 tablespoon grated semi-sweet chocolate

Fill pie crust with blended mixture. Bake at 325° for 20-25 minutes or until crust begins to brown. Remove from oven. Finish cooking filling in microwave for 5 minutes, checking every 2 minutes. The center of filling should be set. Cool pie. Finish with topping. Garnish with chocolate shavings.

Total Carbs = 81

12 Servings = 6.75 carbs each

Lemon Custard Tartlett

Whisk together in medium mixing bowl:

    1 small pkg instant lemon pudding

    2 cups milk

    1 8 oz. block cream cheese (softened)

    1/4 cup sweetened lemonade drink powder

Whip with electric mixer until thickened.

Drop:

    1 vanilla wafer into bottom of custard cups or stand alone decorative muffin cups.

Spoon custard equally into 8-10 cups, depending on size.

Garnish with:

    spoonful of canned lemon custard

Chill completely before serving.

Yield: 8-10 Servings

LEMON COCONUT TARTLETT
Low-Carb Version

Prepare Cream Cheese Pastry (pg 53). Form into ball, chill in refrigerator.
Combine in blender:

     4 eggs
     1/4 cup melted butter
     1/4 cup lemon juice
     1 teaspoon coconut extract
     1 cup Whey-Low powdered

Reserve to garnish:

     unsweetened coconut

Divide pastry dough into 8 equal balls and press into individual tart pans. Pour batter into shells. Bake at 350° for 8-10 minutes or until knife inserted in center comes out clean. Serve with whipped cream.

Total Carbs = 40
8 Servings = 5 carbs each

PUMPKIN PIE

Prepare pie pastry (pg. 52)
(or use purchased pie shell).
Combine in food processor:

    1 small can pumpkin pie filling

    8 oz. cream cheese

    1 teaspoon pumpkin pie spice

    2 eggs

    1 can sweetened condensed milk

Reserve to garnish:

    Whipped cream

Fill unbaked pie shell. Bake 350° for 45 minutes or until edges of pastry begin to turn brown. Remove from oven, place in microwave for 2-3 minutes or until knife tip put in center comes out clean.

Yield: 8-10 servings

PUMPKIN PIE
LOW-CARB VERSION

Prepare 9" Cream Cheese Pastry (page 53).
Combine in blender:

- 1 small can pumpkin (not pie filling)
- 8 oz. cream cheese
- 1 teaspoon pumpkin pie spice
- 4 eggs
- 1 cup Whey-Low (powdered)

Reserve to garnish:

- Whipped cream

Fill unbaked pie crust with pumpkin mixture. Bake at 350° for 50 minutes or until knife inserted in center comes out clean.

Total Carbs = 101
8 Servings = 12.65 carbs each

Coconut Pie

Olivia says:

This is the old 'magic' pie that makes its own crust. You can make it gluten free by substituting gluten free bake mix.

Cream together:

    1/2 cup butter - softened

    3/4 cup sugar

Beat in:

    4 eggs

    1-1/2 teaspoon vanilla extract

Combine and add to creamed mixture:

    1 cup pancake bake mix (Bisquick, Krusteaz, Pioneer)

    2 cups milk

Add and mix well:

    1 cup flaked coconut plus 1/2 cup to garnish

Pour mixture into 9" pie plate prepared with spray oil. Bake at 350° for 50-55 minutes or until knife inserted in center comes out clean. Garnish with coconut. Serve chilled with whipped cream.

Yield: 8 slices

COCONUTTY PIE
LOW-CARB VERSION

For a 9" deep dish pie shell combine:
>   1 cup pecan meal
>   1 cup Whey-Low powdered
>   1 cup unsweetened coconut
>   2 egg whites (save yolks for filling)

Mix into a soft dough. Press into pie dish that has been prepared with spray oil. NOTE: This is easier to do if you place a sheet of parchment baking paper on top and press in place, then remove the paper.

For filling mix until smooth:
>   8 oz. cream cheese
>   1/2 cup heavy whipping cream
>   1/2 cup sugarfree vanilla syrup
>   1/2 cup Whey-Low (powdered)
>   2 egg yolks plus 3 whole eggs
>   1 teaspoon coconut extract

Add:
>   1 cup unsweetened coconut

Reserve for garnish:
>   1/2 cup unsweetened coconut

Fill pie shell with mixture. Bake at 325° for 45-50 minutes or until toothpick comes out clean from center. While still warm sprinkle with remaining unsweetened coconut.

Total Carbs = 144
12 Servings = 12 carbs each

APPLE COBBLER

Toss together until well mixed:

    5 cups peeled sliced apples
    3/4 cup sugar
    2 tablespoons all purpose flour
    1/2 teaspoon ground cinnamon
    1/4 teaspoon salt
    1/4 cup water
    1 teaspoon vanilla

Spoon mixture into a deep 9" pie dish. Dot with:

    1 tablespoon butter - softened

Combine in separate bowl:

    1/2 cup all purpose flour
    1/2 cup brown sugar
    1/2 teaspoon baking powder
    1/4 teaspoon salt
    2 tablespoons butter

Spoon batter over apple mixture in 9 equal portions (batter will spread during baking. Bake at 375°
for 35-40 minutes or until crust is golden brown.

Yield: 8-10 servings

APPLE COBBLER
LOW-CARB VERSION

Toss together until well mixed:

    5 cups peeled sliced apples
    3/4 cup Whey-Low powdered
    2 tablespoons tapioca flour
    1/2 teaspoon ground cinnamon
    1/4 teaspoon salt
    1/4 cup sugarfree vanilla syrup

Spoon mixture into a deep 9" pie dish. Dot with:

    1 tablespoon butter - softened

Combine in separate bowl:

    1 cup almond flour (or pecan flour is good too)
    1/2 cup Whey-Low brown
    1/2 teaspoon baking powder
    1/4 teaspoon salt
    2 tablespoons butter

Spoon batter over apple mixture in 9 equal portions (batter will spread during baking. Bake at 350°
for 35-40 minutes or until crust is golden brown.

Total Carbs = 170
12 Servings = 15 carbs each

Rum Pound Cake Pops

Cream together:
>1/4 cup butter (1/2 stick)
>3/4 cup milk
>2 eggs

Beat in:
>1 box pound cake mix (I used Betty Crocker)
>1 teaspoon rum extract (or 2 tablespoons rum)

Make Meema's glaze substituting powdered sugar for Whey-low or use
>Wilton Treat Glaze Cup (1 container covers 20-24 pops).

Spoon batter into cake pop molds prepared according to directions on pop molds. Bake at 350° for 18-20 minutes. Allow to cool then refrigerate until chilled completely before separating and trimming excess if necessary. Push pop sticks into each.
Follow directions on Wilton Glaze cup to heat glaze. Stir in 1/2 teaspoon rum extract.
Coat chilled pops with heated glaze and decorate with sprinkles or leave plain.

Yield: 30-40 pops (Note: cake pop molds vary but usually make 20 per mold)

Rum Pound Cake
Low-Carb Version

> LIFE IS UNCERTAIN.
> EAT DESSERT FIRST.
> ~ERNESTINE ULMER

Mix together in blender:
- 1 cup butter (2 sticks) softened
- 5 eggs
- 8 oz. cream cheese
- 1/2 cup sugarfree vanilla syrup
- 1 teaspoon rum extract

Mix batter together with:
- 2 cups almond flour
- 1 cup Whey-Low powdered
- 1 teaspoon baking powder

Reserve for glaze:
- 1 cup Whey-Low powdered
- 1/2 cup butter - softened
- 1 teaspoon rum or rum extract
- enough water to liquefy and smooth - add by tablespoon

Pour batter into bundt pan prepared with spray oil. Start in cool oven. Bake at 325° for 1 hour 25 minutes. Remove to cool. Turn onto serving plate. Drizzle glaze over top.

Total Carbs = 120
12 Servings = 10 carbs each

Almond Tart

Cream together:
>   1/2 cup butter (1 stick)
>   1 cup sugar
>   3 eggs
>   1 teaspoon almond extract
>   1/4 cup sour cream

Beat in:
>   2 cups all purpose flour
>   1/2 cup almond flour
>   1 teaspoon baking powder
>   1 teaspoon salt

Reserve for icing:
>   1 cup powdered sugar
>   1/2 cup butter - softened
>   1 teaspoon vanilla extract
>   food color

Pour batter into bottom release tart pan prepared with spray oil. Bake at 325° for 35-45 minutes. Remove to cool. Release tart to serving plate. Pipe icing onto top through pastry tube.

Yield: 12 servings

Almond Tart
Low-Carb Version

Cream together:
> 1/2 cup butter (1 stick)
> 1 cup Whey-Low powdered
> 3 eggs
> 1 teaspoon almond extract
> 4 oz. cream cheese

Beat in:
> 2 cups almond flour
> 1 teaspoon baking powder
> 1 teaspoon salt

Reserve for icing:
> 1 cup Whey-Low powdered
> 1/2 cup butter - softened
> 1 teaspoon vanilla extract
> food color
> slivered almonds (optional)

Pour batter into bottom-release tart pan prepared with spray oil. Bake at 325° for 35-45 minutes. Remove to cool. Release tart to serving plate. Pipe icing onto top through pastry tube. Top with slivered almonds.

Total Carbs = 120
12 Servings = 10 carbs each

Red Velvet Cake

Beat together:

    4 eggs

    1 oz. red food color

    1/2 cup vegetable oil

    1 cup sour cream

Add in:

    1 box yellow cake mix

    1 package instant vanilla pudding mix

    1 tablespoon unsweetened cocoa powder

Reserve for icing:

    1 cup cold milk

    8 oz. cream cheese

    1 box instant vanilla pudding mix

    8 oz. frozen whipped topping, thawed

Pour batter into 9X13 bake dish prepared with spray oil. Bake at 350° for 35-45 minutes. Cool. Mix icing and spread on top. Keep refrigerated.

Yield: 12 servings

RED VELVET CAKE
LOW-CARB VERSION

Beat together:

> 4 eggs
> 1 oz. red food color
> 1-1/2 cup vegetable oil
> 2 teaspoons vinegar
> 1 teaspoon vanilla
> 8 oz. cream cheese

Add in:

> 2 cups almond flour
> 1 cup Whey-Low powdered
> 1 tablespoon unsweetened cocoa powder
> 1 teaspoon baking soda
> 1 teaspoon salt

Reserve for icing:

> 8 oz. cream cheese
> 1 cup Whey-Low powdered
> 1 teaspoon vanilla extract
> heavy cream added by tablespoons until creamy

Pour batter into two cake pans prepared with spray oil. Bake at 350° for 30-40 minutes. Cool. Mix icing and spread on top of one layer then add second layer. Finish frosting. Drizzle sugarfree chocolate syrup for garnish (optional) Keep refrigerated.

Total Carbs = 133.50
16 Servings = 8.5 carbs each

APPLE CARAMEL CAKE

OLIVIA SAYS:

Sometimes you just need a smaller cake. Using a 6"X4" Wilton springform pan makes a cake that is about half the size of a bundt cake pan.

Mix together in bottom of a 6"X4" Wilton springform pan:
>1/2 cup brown sugar
>1/2 teaspoon cinnamon

Make a single layer evenly over sugar/cinnamon:
>Canned apple slices (Cracker Barrel's Fried Apples are wonderful for this)

Mix together in a medium bowl:
>1 box yellow Jiffy Cake
>1 egg
>1/2 cup water

Place pan on a cookie sheet, it might drip a little. Spread batter evenly over apple layer. Bake at 350° for 30-35 minutes. Cool completely. Invert on serving dish. Garnish with nuts.

Yield: 8 servings

Caramel Apple Bundt Cake
Low-Carb Version

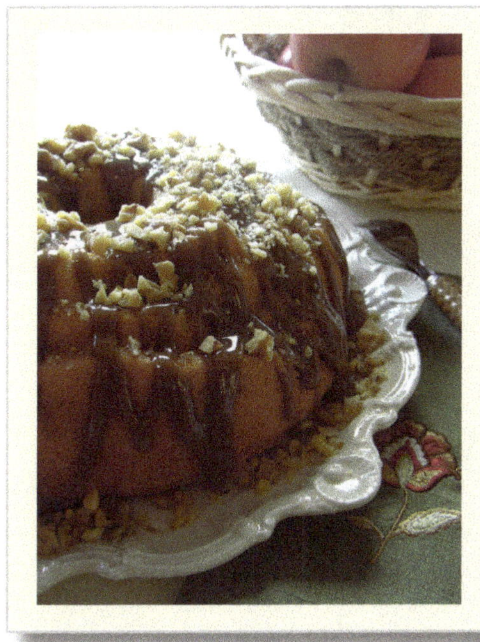

Mix in blender until smooth:
- 8 oz. cream cheese
- 1/2 cup butter (1 stick)
- 4 eggs
- 1/2 cup sugarfree vanilla syrup
- 1 teaspoon vanilla extract
- 1 tablespoon lemon juice

Toss together in separate bowl:
- 1 cup Whey-Low powdered
- 2 teaspoons baking powder
- 1/2 teaspoon salt
- 3 cups almond flour
- 1 cup chopped apples
- 1 cup finely chopped pecans or walnuts

Reserve to make caramel topping:
- 1 cup Whey-Low powdered
- 1/2 cup heavy cream

Fold creamed ingredients into dry and mix well. Spoon mixture into bundt pan that had been prepared with spray oil. Bake at 350° for 50 minutes or until toothpick comes out clean. Cool in pan for 15 minutes then invert on serving plate.

While cake is cooling, make caramel topping by combining Whey-Low and cream in sauce pan, cooking over medium heat until temp comes to 240° (soft ball). Remove from heat. Cool slightly then drizzle over cake. Garnish with chopped nuts.

Total Carbs: 167
16 Servings = 10.46 each

GINGER BREAD CAKEMAN

OLIVIA SAYS:

This is more craft than recipe but you can make your own custom designed cookie/cake mold for all occasions using this fun to do example.

Draw your design onto a piece of parchment paper. Cut it out and place on another sheet of parchment on a cookie sheet.

Soften white Sculpey Polymer Clay and form into 6" strips that are 1-1/2" wide. Fold up one edge 3/4" tall and mold around inside edge of design. Press bottom edge firmly onto the design parchment paper.

Mold small lengths of thin aluminum foil over stand up edge. Fill in center with more aluminum foil. Spray generously with vegetable oil.

Mix any boxed cake or cookie mix of your choice according to directions. I used the Betty Crocker Ginger Bread Cake/Cookie Mix for this Ginger Bread Man. Fill the shape evenly with the batter within 1/4" of the top. Bake at 350° for 20-25 minutes. Allow to cool completely.

Place flat plate, cake board or cookie sheet over cooled cookie. Quickly flip and gently remove mold and aluminum foil. Repeat to flip back to front side.

Decorate as desired.

Yield: Varies depending on design

GINGER BREAD BARS
Low-Carb Version

Cream together until smooth:

    3 eggs

    1/2 cup butter (1 stick)

    1/2 cup sugarfree maple syrup

    1/2 cup Whey-Low brown

Combine in separate bowl:

    2 cups almond flour

    1/2 cup cornstarch

    2 teaspoon baking soda

    1 teaspoon salt

    1 tablespoon ground ginger

    1 teaspoon ground cinnamon

Cream together and reserve for frosting:

    8 oz. cream cheese

    1 cup Whey-Low powdered

    1 tsp vanilla extract

Fold creamed ingredients into dry and mix well. Spread evenly into raised edge jellyroll pan that has been prepared with spray oil. Bake at 350° for 15 minutes or until toothpick comes out clean. Allow to cool, then spread cream cheese frosting and sprinkle with cinnamon. Chill. Cut into bars.

Total Carbs = 138

24 Servings = 5.75 carbs each

OATMEAL MUFFINS

In small bowl mix together:

    1-2/3 cup pancake bake mix

    1 cup quick cooking oats

    1 teaspoon cinnamon

    2/3 cup sugar

Combine in medium bowl:

    1 egg

    1/4 cup vegetable oil

    1-1/3 cup milk

Add dry mix to wet mixture. Stir until blended.

Spoon batter into prepared muffin cups until cups are full. Bake at 350° for 20-25 minutes. Remove from oven and top with garnish of oats, cinnamon, sugar and pecans.

Yield: 6 large muffins

OATMEAL MUFFINS
Low-Carb Version

In medium bowl mix together:
- 2 cups almond flour
- 1/2 cup quick cooking oats
- 1 cup Whey-Low powdered
- 1 teaspoon salt
- 1 tablespoon cinnamon
- 1/2 cup chopped pecans

Combine in separate bowl:
- 4 oz. cream cheese
- 1/4 cup butter

Add:
- 2 eggs
- 1 teaspoon vanilla

Reserve to garnish:
- 3 tablespoons Whey-Low
- 1 tsp cinnamon
- 2 tablespoons oats

Fold all ingredients together just until combined. Spoon batter into prepared muffin cups until cups are 2/3 full. Bake at 325° for 20-25 minutes or until toothpick comes out clean. Sprinkle tops with garnish mixture while muffins are still warm.

Total Carbs = 79
12 Servings = 6.59 carbs each

Lemon Pecan Muffin Drops

In medium bowl mix together:
- 2-1/2 cups bake mix (Bisquick, Krusteaz, Pioneer)
- 2/3 cup sugar
- 2 teaspoons lemon peel, grated (or lemon zest)
- 1/2 cup chopped pecans

Cream together in separate bowl:
- 3 tablespoons butter
- 1 cup milk
- 2 eggs

OLIVIA SAYS:

If you have a muffin top pan, great! But if you don't (Meema is the only one I know who does) just spoon the thick batter onto a cookie sheet like drop biscuits. No special pan needed.

Fold all ingredients together until smooth. Spoon batter like drop biscuits on to cookie sheet that has been lined with parchment paper. Bake at 350° for 12-15 minutes or until toothpick comes out clean.

Top with Lemon Cream Cheese Frosting:
Cream together - 4 ounces cream cheese, 2 Tablespoons butter, 1 cup powdered sugar, 1 teaspoon lemon zest

Yield: 8-10 large muffin tops

LEMON PECAN MUFFIN TOPS
Low-Carb Version

In medium bowl mix together:
- 2 cups almond flour
- 1 cup Whey-Low powdered
- 1 teaspoon baking powder
- 1/2 teaspoon salt
- 1/2 cup chopped pecans

Cream together in separate bowl:
- 1/2 cup butter (1 stick)
- 4 oz. cream cheese
- 2 eggs
- 2 tablespoons lemon juice

Fold all ingredients together just until combined. Spoon batter into muffin top pan that has been prepared with spray oil. Bake at 400° for 20-25 minutes or until tops are golden brown.

Total Carbs = 66
12 Servings = 5.5 carbs each

Pumpkin Bread

In medium bowl cream together:
>1 cup canned pumpkin
>2 eggs
>1/2 cup vegetable oil
>1/2 cup brown sugar

Mix together in separate bowl:
>2 cups Bake Mix (Bisquick, Krustez, Pioneer)
>1 teaspoon pumpkin pie spice
>1 cup trail mix (pumpkin seeds, raisins, nuts)

Fold all ingredients together just until combined. Spoon batter into 1 large loaf pan that has been prepared with spray oil. Bake at 350° for 45-50 minutes or until top is golden brown and toothpick comes out clean from center. Remove to cool slightly, then turn out onto Silpat, waxed paper or wire racks.

Yield: 1 large loaf

Pumpkin Bread
Low-Carb Version

In medium bowl cream together:
- 1 cup canned pumpkin
- 4 eggs
- 8 oz. cream cheese
- 1/4 cup butter - softened

Mix together in separate bowl:
- 2 cups almond flour
- 1/2 cup Whey-Low powdered
- 2 teaspoons baking powder
- 1 teaspoon baking soda
- 1 teaspoon pumpkin pie spice

Reserve for garnish (optional):
- 1/2 cup Whey-Low (powdered) mixed with 4 oz. cream cheese, topped with pecans

Fold all ingredients together just until combined. Spoon batter into 8X8 bake pan that has been prepared with spray oil. Bake at 325° for 45 minutes or until top is golden brown and toothpick comes out clean from center. Cool in pan, then turn out onto serving dish.

Total Carbs = 50
12 Servings (average) = 4.16 carbs each

Banana Nut Bread

In medium bowl cream together:

    1 cup sugar
    1/4 cup shortening

Add:

    2 eggs
    1 cup mashed ripe bananas (2-3)
    2 cups pancake bake mix (Bisquick or other)
    1 cup chopped nuts

Fold all ingredients together just until combined. Spoon batter into 1 large or 2 medium loaf pans that have been prepared with spray oil. Bake at 350° for 50-60 minutes or until tops are golden brown. Remove to cool slightly, then turn out onto Silpat, waxed paper or wire racks.

Yield: 1-2 loaves depending on size of loaf pans

BANANA NUT BREAD
Low-Carb Version

In medium bowl cream together:

    8 oz. cream cheese

    1/2 cup butter (1 stick)

    4 eggs

    1/2 cup sugarfree vanilla syrup

    1 teaspoon banana extract

    1 mashed banana

Mix together in a separate bowl:

    1/2 cup Whey-Low powdered

    3 cups almond flour

    2 teaspoon baking powder

    1/4 teaspoon salt

    1 cup chopped pecans

Fold all ingredients together just until combined. Spoon batter into 1 large or 2 medium loaf pans that have been prepared with spray oil. Bake at 325° for 50-60 minutes or until tops are golden brown. Remove to cool slightly, then turn out onto Silpat, waxed paper or wire racks.

Total Carbs = 80

16 Servings (average)= 5 carbs each

Texas Sheet Cake

Bring to boil in small saucepan and set aside:
- 1 cup brewed coffee
- 1/4 cup cocoa powder
- 1 cup butter

Cream together in small bowl:
- 2 cups all-purpose flour
- 2 cups sugar
- 1 teaspoon baking soda
- 1/2 teaspoon salt

Add and then mix altogether into a smooth batter:
- 1/2 sour cream
- 1 teaspoon vanilla

For frosting:

Bring to boil in saucepan and remove from heat then beat and reserve to frost:
- 3-3/4 cups sugar
- 3 tablespoons baking cocoa
- 1/4 cup milk
- 1/4 cup butter
- 1 teaspoon vanilla

Pour batter into a 11x17 sheet pan that has been prepared with spray oil. Bake at 350° for 20 minutes or until toothpick comes out clean from middle. Frost while still warm.

Yield: 24 slices

Texas Sheet Cake
Low-Carb Version

Bring to boil in small saucepan and remove from heat:
> 1 cup brewed coffee
> 1/4 cup cocoa powder
> 1/2 cup butter
> 4 oz. cream cheese

In medium bowl cream together until smooth with electric mixer:
> 2 eggs
> 2 cups Whey-Low Powdered
> 1 teaspoon vanilla
> 2 cups almond flour
> 1 teaspoon soda
> 1/2 teaspoon salt

Mix all ingredients together with mixer. Pour batter into a 11x17 sheet pan that has been prepared with spray oil. Bake at 325° for 20 minutes or until toothpick comes out clean from middle.

For frosting cream together with electric mixer:
> 2 cups Whey-Low Powdered
> 3 tablespoons cocoa powder
> 1/2 cup butter
> 4 oz. cream cheese
> 1 teaspoon vanilla

Frost while still warm. Chill in refrigerator completely before cutting.

Total Carbs = 72
24 Servings = 3 carbs each

A Word About Artificial Sweeteners

I use several different sweeteners because, for one thing, no one sweetener is perfect for all baking and cooking, except sugar. But since sugar is the primary offending ingredient that contributes to carb count there has to be substitutions for it. The primary sweeteners I use are the newest kids on the block, Sucralose, a non-nutritive (don't you love that term) no-calorie version of sugar and Whey-Low®, a proprietary blend of natural sugars.

Sucralose is marketed under the name of Splenda®. This one (in my opinion)is a vast improvement over either of the long time used and often controversial Saccharin or Aspartame. Unlike its predecessors, Sucralose isn't bitter and it holds up well in heat. But like all artificial sweeteners, Sucralose does not bulk up, preserve or caramelize like the real thing, so these deficiencies must be taken into consideration. And, like all new things that come along that must be proven, Sucralose suffers from some controversy over it's dubious long-term health effects. Aspartame (marketed primarily as Equal®) has been in use since the 1980's and it also continues to be vilified. *I say pick your poison.*

When I published *101 Low-Carb & Sugar-free Dessert Recipes*, I had just discovered the wonders of the sugar alcohol marketed as Maltitol. It seemed at the time to be a perfect substitute for sugar because not only did it not contribute to the net carb count of recipes, it acted very much like sugar especially in candy and cookies. But Maltitol does have its downside, not always but often it can cause lower intestinal distress. And though it is used in an abundance of products now, the end result is hardly worth it. I tried Whey-Low® after fielding so many complaints from people claiming that they couldn't use sugar alcohols and wanted a substitution recommendation from me.

My first experiments with Whey-Low® were instantly encouraging to be as sugar-like in results as Maltitol. By that I mean you can count on the ooey-gooey factor (which cannot be said of Splenda®). Trusting that the processors of Whey-Low® are telling the truth and that their research is accurate, is the leap of faith I chose to make. However, in my experiments, rather than depend on the testimonies from their website: (www.wheylow.com), I solicited real reactions from those whose opinions I knew I could trust. My sister, who was very much adversely affected by sugar alcohols, and her husband, being severely diabetic, made great guinea pigs. Whenever I made a new dessert using Whey-Low®, they tested it for me. My sister had no bad reaction and my brother-in-law had no elevation in blood sugar. That was good enough results for me–if not particularly scientific.

The downside to Whey-Low® is that the net carbs are approximately equal to Splenda®–1 gm per teaspoon–which bumps up the carb counts in my original recipes using the Maltitol.

While we are on the subject, let me add this, I won't even attempt to address in depth all the controversy over artificial sweeteners. My life long base philosophy is–moderation in all things. Sugar isn't good for us either. You can make the very same argument for vitamins as well and we can't live very well without these either. The old adage "too much of a good thing" comes to mind. How about if we just practice some good old-fashioned common sense and exercise a modest amount of reason in what we consume?

Finally, I use Stevia as a sweetening booster. This is really an herb (Sweet Leaf) and has been used for decades, if not centuries, all over the world. A tiny, tiny bit goes a long way but will greatly enhance and balance the super sweetness of the Sucralose especially in the baked recipes. In the resource section I list the Stevia that I personally prefer to use. It is the pure, uncut, carbless white powder and should not be confused with a Stevia Blend, which is a courser mixture of pure Stevia cut with maltodextrin which, by the way, adds a carb to every teaspoon, just as it does in Splenda®.

Many people do not like Stevia. I believe this is because they haven't figured out the best way to use it. Most of my recipes include the Stevia only as an additive and not the base sweetener. When used this way, the Stevia leaves no taste of its own in the finished dish but it does enhance the sweetness while allowing for the reduction of the amount of Splenda or Whey-Low used. This helps keep down the carbs too. As I men-

tioned, there is nearly a carb in every teaspoon of Splenda® so even one-half cup of granulated is equal to approximately 19 carbs. The Sugarfree Syrups sweetened with Sucralose, that I use liberally, claim to be carb-free. I assume this is because the maltodextrin is omitted.

One last note: I subscribe to the "Effective Carb Count" method, which deducts the fiber count in a food from the total carbs. This seems not only logical and reasonable to me, it falls right in line with the same rationale I use in trusting those highly educated folks who tell me I can consume artificial sweeteners without doing irreversible damage to my health.

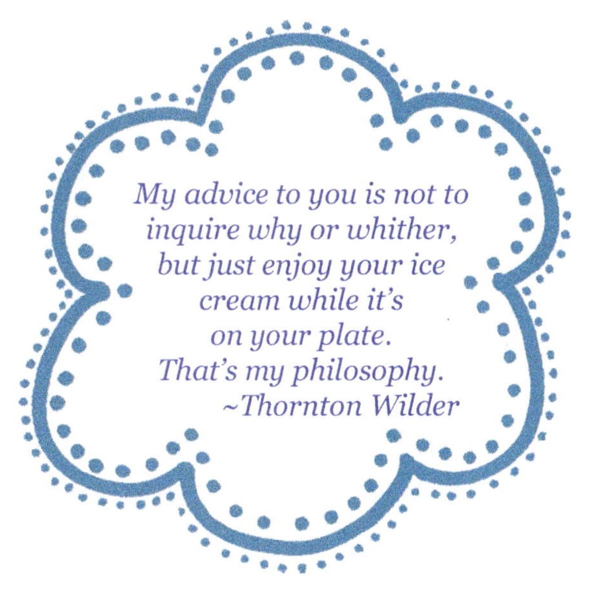

Low-Carb Products

During the height of the most recent Atkins diet craze, the low-carb product market soared because of hype-induced demand, but as the frenzy subsided, many of those start-up companies failed and their products were suddenly no longer available. Thus I found myself inundated with emails from folks looking for substitutions for the Keto products I used in my recipes.

But employing the smallest amount of creativity, making substitutions is not difficult. Let us remember that when Atkins first introduced his diet in the 70's the only "low-carb" product available was Sweet-N-Low. Low-carbing, either as a diet or a life-style is not a challenge. For the most part, those who found it restrictive and hard to maintain were likely doing it wrong anyway. And yes, low-carbing can be done improperly, just as calorie-counting and low-fat dieting can fail because of misinterpretation and misapplication.

The best place to find low-carb products is the Internet and the next best place is at your local health food store and some major grocery chains are still stocking a limited selection of low-carb products in their Health Food aisle. If you are a faithful shopper at certain stores, they will gladly special order or even start carrying some products on request. No doubt, low-carb is still more expensive than foods that are processed with sugar (and high-fructose corn syrup). Sugar is abundant and cheap. Fresh, whole foods are expensive because they are more perishable, thus have shorter shelf-life and are in smaller supply.

Comparing the attitudes of those for and against low-carbing as a nutritional life-style from the first go-round in the 1970's to the second go-round twenty-five years later in the late 1990's to early 2000's, one glaring truth emerged that echoes above and beyond the rhetoric and debate, empty carbs do us as much harm as fat. Even the American Diabetes Association has adopted new guidelines for diabetics which includes carb counting. The new food pyramid came about because of the controversy over carbohydrates in the diet which Dr. Atkins fearlessly pointed out on numerous occasions and to hostile if respected food experts who finally gave in to the empirical evidence. Even though the new Food Pyramid is arguably a compromise, it is more realistic than the previous one. Change never comes without great struggle.

Regardless of the often unkind and negative opinions of Dr. Atkins as a food scientist, he did fearlessly question status quo and pioneered a new direction of thought on the topic of human nutrition and we have to grant him that.

The products on the following page should be staples in a low-carber's pantry–just as flour and sugar are in a standard pantry–and can be found in a number of places. Try the Internet first. If you type in "low-carb" in any search engine, you will come up with hundreds of sites that still sell these and other low-carb, low-sugar or sugarfree products.

Stevia (Now brand)
Available at most health food stores
Splenda®
Available everywhere

Whey-Low® (Granular, Brown & Powdered)
www.wheylow.com

Nature's Flavors Sugarfree Syrups
(many wonderful flavors)
www.naturesflavers.com

Davinci Gourmet Sugarfree Syrups
Available at most grocers in the coffee aisle

Unsweetened Kool-Aid® powder
Unflavored Gelatin
Spice Islands 100% Bourbon Vanilla
(no sugar added)
Lucky Leaf Brand Lite Cherry or Apple Filling
Available at most grocers

Unsweetened Coconut
Macadamia Flour
Pecan Meal
Almond Flour
www.nuts4u.com

Almond Flour
www.lucyskitchenshop.com

Paraffin wax (Gulf Wax)
Available with canning supplies

Vital Wheat Gluten
www.truefoodsmarket.com

Xanthan Gum
www.bobsredmill.com

Food Grade Cocoa Butter
www.oilsbynature.com

Sugarfree Chocolate Buttons
www.bulkfoods.com

Whey Protein Isolate (unsweet, unflavored)
Available at most health food stores

Almond Butter & Sugarfree Peanut Butter
Available at most health food stores

One of the best, most completely stocked Internet resource for low-carb and sugarfree products: Low-Carb Connoisseur
www.low-carb.com

A Word About Nut Flour
Almond, pecan, macadamia and other nut flours are not actually flour at all. Nuts, blanched and processed into a fine, dry meal is 100% nut and are wonderful and nutritious substitutes for wheat flour in most recipes. Please note that nut flour does not contain gluten, a key element in wheat flour, and there are certain other subtle differences in performance and should be combined with other ingredients for the same results that wheat flour gives in baked goods.

CALCULATING CARBS

Please be aware the carbs listed at the end of each recipe is not an absolute. For one thing, there are hidden carbs in many ingredients that I cannot control. Vanilla is one of those sneaky carb adders that you don't think about. Many vanilla extracts list as their first ingredient, sugar. While it is arguable that a teaspoon of vanilla can't add much of anything it does add to the total count. The first thing a carb-counter learns is that carbs add up faster than calories sometimes.

Also, our food manufacturers/processors have guidelines that they use that are set by the Federal Food and Drug Administration. These guidelines put calculations for content into tolerances. Thus, a tablespoon of cream is listed as zero carbs. But that is because the whole pint carton is divided into "servings" and if the serving size holds a trace of carb, it doesn't have to be listed. But if you think you can use the whole pint of cream and not have carbs, you would be wrong. One cup of heavy cream has seven carbs. These do count! An egg has a trace of carb, but if a recipe calls for ten eggs, well, you get my point.

So, what I have done is estimate the total carbs based on the ingredients and divided by the average number of servings. I list the total number of carbs and then the per serving number. I do this because some people like to determine their own serving size. My son-in-law believes that one-half of a Cherry-Cheesecake is a fair serving size. It does no good to point out to him that just because a dessert is sugar-free and low-carb doesn't mean you can eat the whole thing in one day and not impact your weight. I only mention this as a note of warning to those who might lose their focus once they actually taste the Cherry Cheesecake (page 61).

CONVERTING RECIPES TO LOW-CARB

After comparing a few recipes in this collection, it should be fairly clear that converting recipes to low-carb is more than simply substituting ingredients. This is because cooking is a science as well as an art and recipes are actually formulas.

Without delving too deeply into the technical reasons that sugar, eggs and flour can be mixed together and produce a cake, it can be said that certain elements, when combined and heated will bond, congeal and expand. But other elements, of similar construction can also be combined—and produce nearly identical results. Thus you can bake a cake without flour like the Rum Cake on page 75. But you have to add other elements to make this happen.

I do not pretend to be a food scientist but I have learned that the proteins in eggs, cream cheese and almond flour will bond, congeal and rise to make a cake that replicates any pound cake made with flour. Fearless experimentation is the key. My Peanut Butter Cookie recipe (page 11) was my first accidental success when I began this journey. It worked.

That's really all I need to know.

ABOUT THE AUTHORS

Olivia Hoey is working toward a degree in Physical Therapy at Georgia State University which leaves her even less time than ever before to enjoy her love of cooking, but, as we say, she's almost got it so . . .

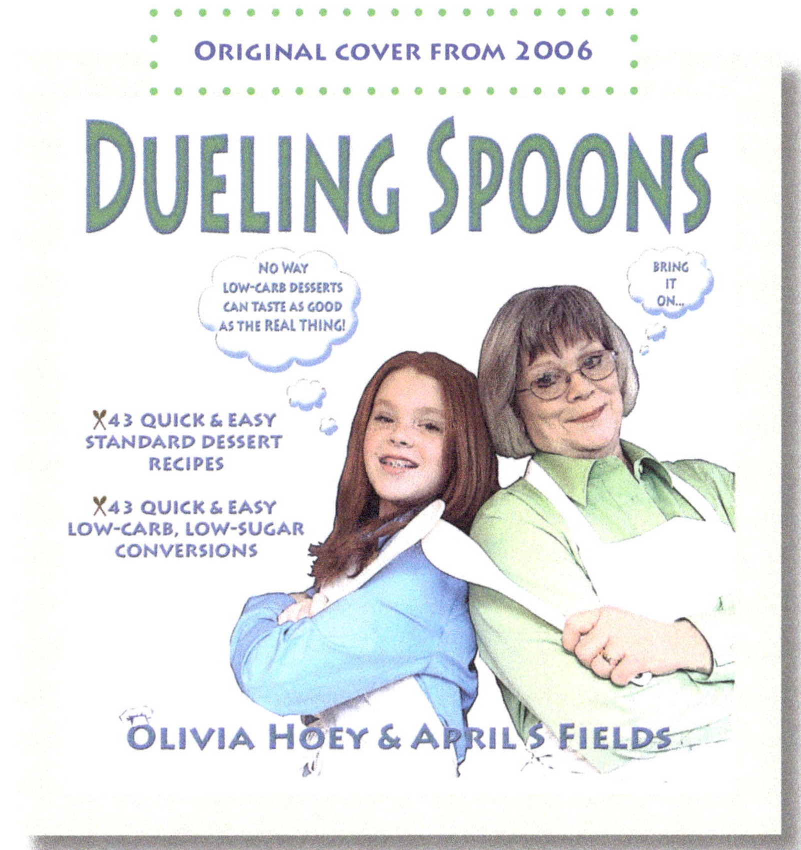

April S. Fields (Meema) is starting to commence to begin to think about retiring, although she finds some things are easier to retire from than others. Writing and cooking seem to be less strenuous activities than building two-story play forts and large furniture.

Making dessert is a life-long calling.

www.ingramcontent.com/pod-product-compliance
Lightning Source LLC
Chambersburg PA
CBHW041035050726
47599CB00018B/1974